Big Breath of a Wish

Big Breath of a Wish

Richard Harrison

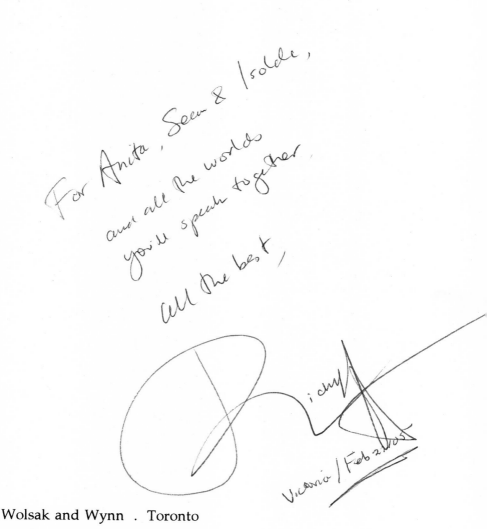

Wolsak and Wynn . Toronto

Typeset in Palatino, printed in Canada by
The Coach House Printing Company, Toronto

Front cover photograph: Richard Harrison
Cover design: James Baillies, Shannon Kilvington and Richard Harrison
Back cover photograph: Lisa Rouleau

Some of these poems, or earlier versions, have appeared in the journals *Arc*, *Ariel*, *Blue Buffalo*, *Everyman*, *filling station*, *Mattoid*, *Prism International*, and *Rampike*; in the chapbook *Calendric*, and in the League of Canadian Poets' anthology, *Vintage 96*.

The author and the publishers acknowledge the support of the Canada Council for the Arts for our publishing program. We also thank the Ontario Arts Council for its support.

The author wishes to thank the Markin-Flanagan Distinguished Writers Programme at the University of Calgary for the Writer-in-Residency which allowed much of this book to be written. Thanks also to the Alberta Foundation for the Arts for their further support of this project.

Wolsak and Wynn Publishers Ltd.
Don Mills Post Office Box 316
Don Mills, Ontario, Canada, M3C 2S7

Canadian Cataloguing in Publication Data

Harrison, Richard, 1957-
  Big Breath of a Wish

Poems.
ISBN 0-919897-62-2
I. Title.

PS8565.A6573B53 1998   C811'.54   C98-932223-8
PR9199.3.H3486B5 1998

Second Printing

For Emma

CONTENTS

The space of writing does not open like a door even though it is the eve of your first birthday and the windows of our city shimmer tonight like candles waiting for the big breath of a wish. We videoed your birth, your mother and her midwives and I together in the bedroom of our house; we thought of our first present to you as the address of your birthplace, the familiarity of your first bed. You were stuck in transition for a long time. I tell you this not to exact a price but because of the way my eyes were opened on your mother that day; away from where she groaned in the bedroom we took ourselves aside and discussed a C-Section, the trip to the hospital unless or if. I admired her also the way I admire athletes, exerting herself for a purpose — we used this language to prepare ourselves — those groans were the groans of a woman who did not allow the body to stop her. But I find it hard, almost impossible, to watch the video now; it unshields me in a way I did not think it would, in a way being there, holding her, then you, did not. When I say I will write this, she tells me, *remember how she was born because they lost the sound of her heart, why I had to push so hard and fast, tearing skin because of that silence.* May this always be a gift we give; we could not wait to hear you.

B'da B'da B'da B'da bird beak heart, woodpecker heart, o yes, *beat beat beat beat beat beat beat* this is you child, turtle, your first sound assurance *m'here m'here m'here.* Stein says, there is no such thing as repetition, every *tap tap tap* a new word made newer in the speaking — *b'da b'da b'da:* the way John Lennon spat-sang *Buddha* from the list of those in whom he did not believe. He sang *I believe in me,* then added, *Yoko and me;* Lisa smiles big, the stethoscope in her ears a caliper of that smile, midwife pressing the small steel drum of its ear to her belly, your heart singing *b'da b'da b'da;* growing, birdwings, your little long life, no such thing as repetition *again again again.*

This is about staying up with a crying baby thinking *o lucky us, we have a colicky baby,* staying up till 1 or 2 or 3 each night with a baby we thought we couldn't stop crying except by rocking for hours at a time, every mother helping us with the proper rocking motion, me staying up with Emma screaming scream scream scream — this is us thinking that breastfeeding came naturally and our baby was shrinking, each night reversing the womb, the neat round layer of fat that filled her slick skin when she squeezed out all spry and rounded like a rubber raft; this is how we didn't hear, how babies aren't supposed to *say* anything, even when they are crying, what everyone tells us to expect — *hey, babies cry* — me watching the Leafs from the West coast while Emma passes out on my chest, I pass out on the couch, and another team with all its talent on paper loses where it counts ... this is how we hate our children, we do not listen, our baby's first word was *waaaaghahaaaagghaaahhhhh* a tale you can tell was told to idiots because we thought it signified nothing.

Tonight you are lying along my forearm, your neck over my wrist,
your head in my palm. This is the way my father holds me in my
favourite picture of my father and his firstborn son though you are
my firstborn daughter and starving in my hands; tonight I slide a
tube the width of a vein across my fingerprint into your shrunken
mouth, and you are drinking the milk your mother pumped from
her breasts and suck by suck we are keeping you out of hospital,
we are keeping you alive. You will thrive as they say, the flesh will
fill again on your body, and your vocabulary will burgeon
outwards from the persistent word for hunger we could only hear
and did not hear, so thick the veil around us; there are other cases
like yours, like ours, in the literature. Soon you will sleep your first
night through, and when you read this, years from now, do not be
fooled by the word "tonight." All poetry is reflection and every
location travelled there is reached by language, the only vehicle we
have to move like silk through wounds our bodies forget. Fact is,
the book is done. I cannot erase the shame I have for your hunger,
or the language I use to describe it. The young woman who coos at
you now, then comments as if you were some kind of dare, "I'm
not ready to be a parent" is thinking only of what you take, the
way we were thinking beneath our own desire for you. I too have
wrapped a gauze around the movies I've missed, the parties
unattended, bars unvisited. This is the script for the adult world
where *baby* = *disaster*. Fact is, no one is ready, the blood at my wrist
is weary in its blue filament, but if you asked me when I was
doing what I wanted to do most, I'd say this, now, holding your
head, feeding you her milk in turn with your mother in the middle
of the night, your mouth at the end of my lifeline.

There you lie on the change table, tummy naked as a nickel.
I tickle you, blow raspberries, and you laugh your baby
just learning to laugh laugh — glA! Naturally I think of Derrida,
your burble the name of his notorious book; all the way from the other
side of meaning, he is undoing everything you do today, and
it's not easy, either. But of his works the one I think of as
describing us is +R, which I do not know how to voice as a single
sound, so I say *tr*, a sound you cannot make, or "plus R."
And R is my initial: me enlarged by you on the side where R seems
final but waits for an eye to open it like the left hand margin of the poem.
Or it's the sign for your Dad in the bargain
dressing you beside the illustrated alphabet, cut-out pictures
of baby faces, lions & the Riddler with his serpent mark of a question —
each of these in its novelty made you stare and wave your arms and
coo before I hung them on the wall. *Plus R* is the text with a sketch
at the crux — not words, a drawing — a huge fish caught
at the oblique limit of sea and air on the hook of human skill,
whose gills and wrinkled lip and suspension by
an unseen hand imply all you have to learn about
the bait, the struggle, the extended arm, the end. But listen —
out of that upraising silver mouth, the water far behind — a baby laughs.

Ba! Ghhhhhhhh Aaghoooo, aahghoo......preword sounds already
I spell in English. Preworded speaker with her very own face, Emma
looking down from the flying cradle my hands make
so her fat cheeks plump forward and she could be a balloon with eyes,
and oh that smile from up *Hi There!* big drool bomb baby gob smile —
I accept her love the way punk musicians take spit from their fans:
whatever made her mouth used mine: *aahgooh* is *good, aah,*
is *you,* easy glottal hello, hello, hello again.

Emma is learning to growl: a tremble primitive,
or machine; a below-language sound,
tiger outside the cave, pussycat in your ear,
lawnmower on the first suck of the gas.
Orbison (they begged and applauded him
do the growl, Roy). Sounds like she's working on
the big wet one says everything functions as it should:
good news, fossil pattern, apish grip,
vocabulary, *grrrrrr, grrrrrrr, grrrrrrrr*.

Emma is burning to grow a body primitive,
a machine below language,
cypher outside the word, feminine in your ear;
the neighbour has his two-year-old son
give her *her first official kiss from a guy.*
Other (the pink horizon festooned
be a good girl). Sounds like she's working on
the big wet one says everything riots as it should:
good news, broken pattern, human grip,
vocal body, *grrrl, grrrrl, grrrl.*

She
turns
her head
into a boom box, bagpipe,
Hunnnh.....hunnnhnhm....hunnnnhmh
the song of
the forced
smile
on the lips
of the balloon
belugas in the St Lawrence
squeezing air from sinus to sinus in the skull —
a leap of sound to test
the distance
in the dark,
bring a bowl
of rice and lentils
across the out-of-reach with the power of her voice
alone in the deep blue
say she begins
to navigate
at breakfast.
yum.

Sound is the soul of the object released.
                                    — John Cage

Before she could put her lips together on purpose,
she found the letter *v* where the corner of
a building block bearing its letters fit
the space of her open-aahhing mouth.

She grips the wood like a harp,
hums *veuvve, veuvve,* and her jaw
grows into sound she uncages from the toy
with the patience of necessity
as language mothers invention.

Emma, I am speaking for you these days, these days they call such work *appropriation*. I am stealing your words before they are words. You make all the sounds for Chinese or Malay or German (or the language of men or the language of women), and I hear you in English, explain the items in the kitchen in English: *This is the fridge, I say, a small room that becomes very cold in order to slow the process of decay.* You feel the feathers of rinky air and make that inward growling *unhnhnhnhnh   unhnhnhnhnh* you make when you hold Mookie or your little cloth clown or the Three of Hearts in both hands; I say it is the sound of thinking, low in the throat, the mind before you pull the mind in.

I open my mouth wider than words (an exercise
from birthing class to understand that vaginal stretch,
the crown emerging through straining skin) (the corners

sting and go numb), and emit
your little seagull cry, the cry even you have lost
by your 4th month. Or tighten my face
and bubble as if at a trumpet the way

you do with the concentration of Picasso who spent
his whole life, he said, attempting the seriousness
of a child at play.

My cry comes out high and wailing; at the purse
my buzzing insistent, mechanical,
and yet from these ghosts in my lips,

you learn your mouth, too,
buzz and bubble,
forth and forth,
eye to eye.

Supported by my hands, Emma walks
the width of the park,
from kitchen to bedroom,
couch to door. She's quit talking: gone
are the multisyllables, the first word candidates.
All she does is *ababababa* —
and she walks. Right now the rest of
the alphabet is not important.
What she cares about
is getting from a to b.

Ba! BawuuuWouuup! Sentences now, full phrases,
swirl of the shimmering seen: our cats, my face, solid
food, paper heroes, a rubber ostrich, Nipper the dog in
his immortal pose of deception receiving through
the crackle of the gramophone, his master. Words
are proof of the music to follow, baby,
this is your speech on the page,
impossible speech in our alphabet (but what poet
has not been told *I didn't understand your work
until I heard you read it.*)

The old 3-d joke gets Emma's biggest laugh these days — Lisa
swinging her in and out of focus: peek-a-boo — *Hooohhhh, aaaahhhh*
comes from deep in her belly — part laugh, part *Hi Mom,* part
thaumazein, a chunk of philosophical wonder — the *Hooohhhh,*
aaaaahhhh from the lungs beneath a high wire; carnival assembles an
audience bored with science, says goodbye! to the flesh, let your
breath travel the leaping distance of your eyes. Hey! I was there at the
birth and still your every laugh is my *hooohhhh, aaaahhhh* at you, baby.

Emma has not spoken for 2 weeks and today she ripped a page in two, one of the photographs of a baby hanging beside the change table — *phhwwp!* Announcement! I lied. She is whining, has whined for the last two weeks, the subtle burbles, coos, birdsong, mammalsong gone elsewhere, replaced by the same constipated grumble as thought but higher in the nose — *uunnnh, uuunnnnnnnnhhhh:* this is the world, Emma-I-am-me, the long, slow percolation of self into resisting flesh, frustration, your feet slip on the wet embankment, 54 bones, your two hands, work in perfect sync for the first time — the page is clean and torn: here's a word from the split head of that child, the first word in the articulating vocabulary of muscle.

The world goes in
piece by piece where
words come out
to name it —

the face of
a tongue-loved doll,
a duck,
a spinning bird. I fold

my lips around my teeth
and press a rattle there
to find in me Emma's own
rush to extract
all there is to know

with the hard tack of her gums.
There's a dull ache
you don't feel every day,
and I surprise myself
with too much

memory
to do anything but
mime the way it looks,
the way the world,
as new as good,

urges itself into a mouth,
impresses itself
on the palette of a tongue,

and it will be too soon when,
all blended in a flock of words,
it comes from her a calling.

When it comes from her a calling
all blended in a flock of words,
it will be too soon.

The world impresses itself
on the palette of a tongue,
urges itself into a mouth
as new as good.

The way the world
mimes the way it looks
is memory

and too much surprise
you don't feel every day.

There's a dull ache
with the hard tack of her gums
to extract all there is to know
in Emma's own rush
to press a rattle there.

My lips around my teeth
I fold a spinning bird
a duck,
the face of
a tongue-loved doll
to name it —

words come out
piece by piece where
the world goes in.

So we let her try *WordPerfect*, and Emma hits

m

her first letter, name's heart with its double beat, the way we sign her
name to her, fist closed with three fingers over the thumb, the
newborn grip. And about the only thing she says these days. She's
given up on the subtleties of mouth and tongue, every language on
earth spoken all at once: she's taken to the solitary phoneme, the
narrow, piercing *mmmmmmm,mmmmmmmm* of hunger, desire, fatigue.
She's figured what works.

She types another *m*.

On the screen, *mm* & Emma

is silent as she does this.

Then she hits zero, the meeting of alphabet and number line, the null,
the cry, nothing, *0,O*,

Em em oh. And then,

an *m* again, Emma rocking back and forth in Lisa's arms, Lisa looking
at the screen; I'm someone saying to their partner at the Ouija board,
C'mon, you're moving it. I was looking for the random text, a fragment
of the collected works of that fabled infinite number of monkeys in
whom I do not believe even if one of them did poke out *the immortal
part of myself.*

But here's my girl in her mother's lap. She brings her wide palm down to the arbitrary signs

and she gets *m .. mm... mm0...*

mm0m

Dear baby, dear heroine, here you live in heaven with everyone I ever
knew, knew me, costumed and ageless. Yesterday I spoke of the
woman I lived with for ten years, helped raise her children, my second
family. It will be incredible for you, that life I had. I had that life. We
were talking about the how, how it began in my therapist's office, the
concoction of younger man and older woman, love so pure, so
misunderstood I told no one about the office, sleeping with a mother
— go figure, my days self-flattering under the hood of the false: this is
what is not for you, not for you at my hands, not for you at the hands
of others. You can be set up for it, wanting and wanting, pleading
eyes, bottomless pit, bad body. You can want something like incest.

Now I know in part, the motto of my alma mater, and the passage it is
from continues *I see through a glass darkly.* I turn the monitor back on,
and the dark glass turns to light and the words I wrote when I could
not see them say *I have respect for war, for what it must have taught my
father about no going back, this is like what you are teaching with your birth,
and I couldn't have known that about my father until I saw your mother
push you from her belly, heard your gasp, cry like old metal.* And this
image, rising to me from the memory of the machine, these words
shock me for the easy transition between war and birth I have
denounced so often in the works of other men. But I have never seen a
peaceful death, and my father never saw me born or my brother born:
these are the ballsy ignorances I bring. What I know firsthand is there
are people I loved who hate me now, some things no hero can undo,
how you just have to learn to carry on and think well of yourself,
endlessly well — *this I want to teach.* This morning you scaled the wall
behind our bed, found your face in the tinted mirror there and kissed
it. I wrote this, too, into the blind plate, and as I wrote it, I looked into
the darkened glass for what stared back, waiting for me to know.

You bathe with me as a child I (re)write, and
there we are & the earlier words of *my father's body* lie
beneath us like a map of the world. I trace *enormous limbs,*
giant hand, huge cock at rest in the water;
8 months old (already!) and your research
takes me back: *I bathed with him as a child,*
I wrote, *my father, naked,*
and I was naked and small in his silence.

Between my shins and feet, you explore the surface
of tubwater, push your wide hand down like a fin;
the water closes, breaks while your fingers rise and
sound the mysteries of new and basic information: up, down,
above, below, my unremarked flesh beside you.

There are things you will know only too late, but not
how the scars came to my body, not how I sleep with your mother.
At 38 here I am, the father, and you are reaching down for
my penis which you have noticed for the very first time; you reach
beneath the line of water and air once itself a wonder
now transparent in your newfound knowledge.

I turn you away saying *no, no,* gently,
like it was a prank, *nooo, no my girl,*
though all I knew then was you cannot touch me
because you cannot touch me.

In the quiet rewriting it hits
like a crack in *the home planet* — the word
I use to mark the territorial limit of my skin in our ocean
stretched out on the couch of the bath,
the word I use is no,
the death inside me, growing; too much has happened,
and the feminine begins in you when I say *no*
over this inert little flesh, this masculine you cannot touch,
immense with all it has done.

Queen Emma imitates the cat; beside
my cheek her infant gaze becomes
the eyes of Conscience in an illuminated
Bible or a Saturday cartoon
who whispers beside a tempted ear.
For those eyes I must come clean —
acquit myself, pay my taxes and the rent, write
what I need a lawyer's help to write,
get back what's mine and taken,
take my steps toward the daily braveries
I have put off but were always
there before me. And before me there
was my father & the distance
between what he said and what he was &
one day that way, too, I shall be seen,
my name where now she chimes out *da*
da when I point to my chest and ask
who's this? You might ask, does she know
she *speaks*? And half of me says yes,
names all jumbling with animal sounds —
in her vocabulary a sheep is always *Bbaaaa*
and how now a cow
is merely *Mmmouuuu*. But
science always reveals itself
as Romance over time, and this
is my observation:
Meeya, meeya, said Emma, and
the cat fell quiet
as if the baby stole its breath.

1. The head

*Look at this sketch of Captain America. Notice that he's eight and three
quarters heads tall. If we draw a hero he's got to look like a hero — he should
be of heroic proportions. Unfortunately, the normal six and a half head tall
proportions would make him seem somewhat dumpy.*

— Stan Lee & John Buscema,
How to Draw Comics the Marvel Way

Emma's head stuffed with senses, sounding board, dictionary, cpu, her
head in my own hand, pure round head, pure angular head, brittle
star of hair at the crown; look at me little head, I have longed for
superheroes who could hold their whole heads in one of their hands,
men always drawn as if you lay on the floor looking up, mouth open
in awe, men whose mouths were big enough only for the dry tail ends
of word balloons, longed to be a baby-head to myself, for men who
are better than the best bodies I have seen, better than Ali, better than
Hull, than Schwarzenegger who has given himself back to the smaller,
sustainable flesh of his marriage and fathered a daughter, better than
my father doing the fifty push-ups he could do when he was the age I
am now, better than any Dad.

2. Cape

The page flutters but not like cloth.
I cannot drape it from my shoulders,
become even more masculine in
the feminine sway of fabric in the breeze,
furling wings. I am dressed in ordinary clothes, and the streets
go unpatrolled by me in the separate darkness
of your infant dreams, my sleep well attended with years of practice.
I have tried in vain to render the cape for even a paper man
but you have spoken yourself into the body of every woman
and I plumb a special cringe I cannot fathom or explain when
a child I cannot save is threatened for our entertainment,
a young girl bared for my arousal. I have no cape, escape from you
or love or any lie I've told. I have this blanket in the morning
and wrap it round you drowsy in the rising sun.

3. Armour

The poem is a kind of armour that removes itself. *Father* surrounds me
as it once did him. I saw through and yet. I will fail what I teach, this
much I've taught myself. Yet it was one of his favourites, Kipling, the
soldier's poet, who wrote of *triumph and disaster, treat these two
imposters just the same*. It only appears less personal to say *Richard loves
Emma*. The *I* I utter at the beginning of the sentence protects me. I
believe in this language the way Crusaders believed in their steel
under the Jerusalem sun. A rude awakening. The smoke from their
pyres still clings to my child in the term *Witches' Milk. Ontology
recapitulates Phylogeny* is a jingle biology students use to say the way
the fetus develops is evolution on fast forward. It is false. But the
language does not forget; *Knight* comes from the German word for
somewhere between young man and a man of proven worth. I hold
my hours-old daughter in my arms, thin clear liquid seeps from her
nipples, its name encasing.

4. Clothing

This is the law of clothing the heroically proportioned flesh — in street clothes the body is smaller than it is dressed in lycra, or when it is naked: the hero *surges* from the cloth: we grow in action and the liquid coverage of drama — diaper time, bath time, nude knees at the beginning, bending beneath the stomach, the beginning of the crawl. Emma-I-am-me announces all these with the first burbling trumpet-mouth *bhububhubbhubbuhb* and on all fours rocks like a drunken hand in the morning. Then, instead of the lunge her eyes have made of the space before them, she falls, face flat, squeaking into the blanket, her fat arms out like the measure of a fossil bird, naked cheek hidden in the cloth, captive like a giant.

5. Disproportion

What's monstrous most excites: Golem, Thing, Hulk, Abomination,
oral tradition in the written world, the Beast cast out of The Republic
by its first Great Book. Fable distorts the chest the way the line of the
poem distorts our speech, negates the teaching of faith through faith in
the word alone. The baby cries, vents, wails her frustrations at the
bolted gate, rocking horse too heavy to lift, the partition of rooms she
attempts to walk through, and, given her experience so far, why not?
Bonk! Beginning with the written word, the power of the chest is how
it makes air take language from mind to mind. The sublime becomes
what cannot be taken in after the senses are loaded full. Then you are
isolated with beauty, and a monster is *defined* as *alone*. I exhale words,
my heroes, family, memories, animals, they leave my chest like flung
gravel and you can hear the writing as it hits the wall.

6. My people

These are the drawings of my childhood and its fantasies. Arms wide
apart, legs dramatic and split, face front, puppet men and women
distinguished by their costumes. Batman wears a mask because he has
no face: if you don't believe me, look at Superman over the years. Dad
painted vivid in oil, drew in black dust, filled the big squares of his
canvasses with a throw of colour like the sound effects of a punch —
rock and sky and water to my left and the hard chests of men in the
right, this is what I grew between. My people always looked straight
ahead, always the same, as distinct and revered as tomb drawings,
hieroglyphs waiting for the stone translation by which the picture
becomes the word out loud. I never drew other than them, and today,
looking at the page I could fill with the lines of a hero in flight or lines
of text, I realize I have never put the figure in motion the way I love
even the failures of speech.

They come back a week before 7 months: the syllables — ragtag, jumble tumble more clearly now I can almost count the letters: today l, y, d, a, and the sounds she makes on the in*hhhhhaaalle* before she learns the inhale is silent: in her mouth she's pushing the wet, stippled muscle of language between her gum and lower lip, waving and tugging in the lip like someone groping in a purse for coin: words if you listen askance, *aoaoaa... ddldll... ya...aaahh!* Then she opens Lisa's mouth with her fingers, smiling, grasping her mother's tongue.

Foreword

The word we wait for is always the first — origin issue, book of hope, opening element in the list of *what she says* and *what we say*, the X in overlapping circles of logic, treasure map, gold in the chest breathed out, the mystery of names in her mouth: over and over we've been saying *food, bird, ma ma, da da, kittykat, bye bye, Emma* introducing introduction; in the end she reaches out, sinks her fist into feline fur, the tape is running and there it is:

The Word

kiddykat.

Afterword

Today Lisa's face is the yellow light of caution when she puts the recorder to her ear, but when she hears it, she smiles and nods and yes it is clearly enough *kittykat* for her, so this is what counts as the first word. But this is not the proof. The proof is this morning the cats jumped up on the bed where Emma was lying with us and each time she saw one she said *kiddykat.* And I find it harder and harder to read into (write over) her since it is she who is re(de)fining the device to take up the sounds she hears us making to make sounds of her own in the fragile lattice of object and sound and speaker (which is always collapsing under discussion). It is the second utterance of *kiddykat* that makes the first one speech which is the way the language travels backwards in time, the future changing the past, and no one can hear the first word until much much later.

Dear Emma. Yesterday in the bookstore I heard a baby cry the
yayayaya you made some months ago when you were learning your
tongue as it rose, humpbacked, against the roof of your mouth. I was
holding a Bible, shopping for the staples, tools of the trade of narrative
and poetry, nothing exhaled being without precedent. I had forgotten
you at this stage, as if you'd always been the 18 lbs I saw you last, had
4 teeth & deep-set eyes neither your mother nor father have in our
heads. As if you were never the sleeping newborn supposed between
us on your first night swaddled like a pupa. You were learning to
breathe that night, and the air you slurped through your nostrils like
the straw that ends the drink was our comfort in the valley of the bed.
When you went silent, having learned in a dormant hour to breathe
the breath beneath this page, I woke up terrified and put my cheek to
your face to listen for your life. The baby in the bookstore learning the
tongue and lungs in concert on the rooftop of his mouth singing
yayaya is hard at work, as you were hard at work and will not
remember. When you finally have language, you cannot imagine
yourself without it. Words backdate themselves. The speaker always
exists. I'm holding *Yaya's* Bible open in the middle. *In the beginning was*
the word is the oldest trick in the book.

Going house to
house, I'm shopping
for our home
among the homes of
others already
here and advertising —
For Sale: 1 Crib.
I look this one over,
admire the wood, check
the distance between
the rails. Then I see that space
between the mattress
and the bars right
down to the metal guts
of lift and lower &
this is not for you
r little fat feet to
puncture when you wake
and rise to stand,
your face just above
the bars in the photos
I carry though I know
it has changed
while I wait for you to join me.
In my last memory
you are reading with me —
attending as I use
a voice behind you
over the words
before us both,
a voice I never use
except with books.

But look at me —
my power
is all in my head —
the camera is cruel
with my arms — it breaks
them off, offers them
back as the bones
of a much larger man.
Every parent carries
the guilt of a near miss —
it was through a space
no wider than this
you rolled off the change
table into the drawer
I'd bowed to open
in the everyday choice
of a morning shirt
for my baby,
a space
no wider than what
the current owner
of this crib
is willing to sell me
as safe — a crack
in time no thicker
than a camerasnap,
and you were there,
fallen
through the vapour
my arms were not
into the miracle of
the drawer being open

enough, just enough,
to make a little crib
for you and with
its armless sleeves
embracing.

After 3 years' absence, I'm back
on the rink. Right now you are too young to
appreciate the irony of steel between
me and a Herculean pond where I forget
everything I ever knew how to do on skates — yes,
I lost all my body once possessed of soaring
a circular breeze among schoolchildren turning
and turning the untiring gyre of a truly Canadian
O. Ms. Harrison Rouleau,
for the part of you from Britain and France, the part
to which we are supposed to bend in literature and speech,
this ice is the perishing of the world.
But here, where knees are bent on a frozen lake
to give power to the moving figure, this ice teaches, this ice
is the birth of play. Here are my hands. You reach up,
grab them and run the only way you know: head forward,
torso like a skater's at the angle of falling,
working the carpet like a pair of footpumps;
you are getting ready for this abandon, this disproportion, and I,
learning how not to think of my body again and just go and go,
I remember.

Out it comes, the new sound — *lurgle* — my daughter in a new
house where one word becomes the whole of speech, her tongue
torqued for the first time around *lurgle lurgle*. She looks up at me from
the floor surrounded by toys like stone chips from a sculpture; *lurgle
lurgle lurgle*, she says showing the underside of her tongue. The books
say this is nothing, a spasm, the not-yet-language of the brain,
grammar without surface, or surface without grammar (who can tell?),
and yet the poem cannot be made, it must be found, *a tune* someone
said, a rhythm, begun before even your hands become your own.

His heart just stopped. What is prayer? I carry on my normal life as if the perfection of every task will somehow make him well. This writing needs an address. I catch myself staring at the leaves the way my weeks-old daughter stared from my arms in the garden, fixedly and without the practice of expression. I argued my way through university with the idea that faith was the ability to believe, a human power alone. Nothing I can do can do anything, yet I stay by the phone, by the page within the shining machine looking for words to bring him back as if persuasion were possible: in prayer in the Ivory Coast I witnessed the sacrifice of a goat, its blood poured over an altar together with other offerings, the blood and fat and a good bottle of scotch mixing in our nostrils to let the dead sleep though the living excavated their corridors. The dead slept and the living went about their work raising and lowering their arms at will. How things are connected is beyond us, even the most familiar. I ask the air to conduct like flesh, whatever keeps my heart beating to reach him. I ask the doctors to be prayerful in their duties, out of all the nothing I can do, for perfect words to make him well.

The best words fall
like the first, sudden droplets of
the way of the world. I want
something written the way a mourner's
mouth craves bread. In the manner of prayer
we have driven miles to be
by him. Of his heart attack
my father-in-law says *The sun is still*
shining and I'm on the right side
of the grass; on the green
of hospital sheets, he emerges from
tubes in his arms and up his nose, he counts himself
blessed in the language of golf.
I want this poem. I want to argue
with experience and the art before me:
here there is no place that does not see you,
no beauty beautifully described,
no human column gazed at
in a gallery ever declared
more clearly than his stricken trunk
You must change your life. Truth is,
the world can bust a man with
a clot of his own blood quick as
flatten a bumper crop with
hail — where is my baby?
her babble and squeal, the tossing
touchstone sound drowned
in my pulse. I know she's been uttering,
laying down the deep tracks of
sentences, the socket-space between brain
and tongue and hunger and sheer
delight: back home she's being bad —

she runs to the breakneck basement stairs,
the chrome-topped garbage can that showed her
her own face then fell on her yesterday
like a trap; she's squealing with laughter at
mother's chase and she's beginning to get the hang
of the way human rules are
broken, the world works without
pause. When she's had her fill
of repetition, she will turn on the laws of nature,
her vocabulary, and ask for
meaning, but she is only beginning
to use her face, and this morning
she plucked a ripe tomato
from her grandpa's garden,
and bit through the skin.

Time to write, fill up a page
           — Ward Maxwell

Time to write, fill up a page. Even if nothing comes of it, it is *the act*,
a motive as pure as the one I ascribe to baby talk, filling the air.
Bulonga bloo, she says, unaccompanied by gesture, by want.

She understands language now but does not use it, so the books say
that do not predict how important independence will be to her by 11
months, so important she shoves the proffered spoon away and will
not eat unless she picks it up from the table herself.

This is my entire argument against *basic need*:
even the hungry must give their consent.

Bulonga bloo. Neither language nor non-language. Time to write,
there is no page: I am working the screen, the light — between the
key and the shape of the letter, a system illiterate as nerves to
their messages of pain or pleasure, hunger, rage.

The page is the screen on pause, words consenting to be still;
all the books talk about what happens when you wean the baby,
when you go back to work, etc. None we read, not one, ever said
one day the baby will just stop, and the story you have been making
with the flow of your milk and her hunger is done and over,
and her mouth, lipping the air for words, says give me nothing,
nothing is the thing I want the most.

Ah! the new page, like a fresh diaper,
the white space next to the body,
rich if everything works as it should. Am I too much
the father, I find some glory
in the firm shit of my child?
So what?

On a day like today when I am jealous
of the better-looking poets in the country,
my baby names the world in me. She says
tDha when she touches a building block
and I am there; she says *Mhu-mhu* when she looks
at Lisa, our two faces shining like
the change from summer light. This is the way
the fall came into our house: her grandfather
pitched nosefirst into the darkness between
the light of day and the light his faith told him waited.
But they did not let him go. Around the October table
we raised our glasses one after the other,
offered our wine to words of thanks —
Dad's alive, Dad, *tDha* —
the syllable everything beautiful without compare
present and at hand.

Emma says
Hi haiei yaoodah hunh
aya kawuhn ay lua
aooha hudlduddle
hahooah oohegg
awahadha hunh
yeahwa budha yeow
yayaba a yay
heyny anowbda

I Spellcheck that.
It comes out

Hi Haiti, ya odd hunk;
aye Kahn am luau
hurl deadly halo, oaf
oh egg, a bad hunch,
yeah, a Buddha eye,
a bad eye
a yak
hey!
an Aeneid.

Or

This is the mirror
that erases the face,
a clear shot
at the back of my head
where balance and sleep
exchange jobs daily.
There's no point smiling
in your infant strategy for love,
this poem cannot look;
but the grown-ups,
hey, they laugh.

Sleeping well in the crib in her own room

Finding her own hair, patting it softly

The last drink from the breast

5 steps in succession

Refusing to be fed, insisting on the spoon

Pulling my hair for comparison

Waving goodbye without tears. *See ya!*

Choosing the correct toy in answer to the question *Where's Kermit?*

Releasing the last handhold, adjusting balance
only with movements of the head

Realizing the humour in it

Reading to herself, sometimes in the dark of the morning

Flipping the heavy pages, murmuring *Buhwah, buhwah*
over words she cannot see

Demanding to be read to, crawling, book in hand

Demonstrating the book as location of performance

Palming the ball

Kicking hard enough to be dangerous

Saying *isshhss, isshhsss* for aquarium fish, pictures of fish,
the word *fish* said in her presence, and a tin of salmon.

When my daughter wakes up she talks to the dark or empty room.
She says *lul lul lul lul* waving her tongue from side to side *lul*ling her
way through the rhythm of the spoken sentence. More and more the
transcripts of what she says read like words; I get up from the chair
holding the paper I've been penning while she slept. I walk down the
hall to her room, she's still *lul lul lul*ling in her crib, and her voice is
calm and quiet, like someone at prayer or reciting to herself.
Sometimes these periods last 5, 10 minutes of peaceful speech, *someone
will come, someone will come.* But the hall is not empty — the door
opens and I walk out and my face is 7 years ago. I am leaving my
former family, and I leave it still believing I love my stepchildren and
they love me. But I have to go, though it will take me several years to
say why. The letter in my hand is another failed attempt at apology.
There is nothing I can ask of them now except forgiveness for what I
had to believe in order to carry on — what we had was not love
because the way we parted kept this baby unborn for years. I am
walking away from the baby who expects someone and the
expectation means the room is empty. Goodbye. I hesitate in the
hallway. Even what you do for your own good can leave you
damaged. I know I could turn around and follow me out of the house,
but the phrase *this baby unborn* won't leave me, either, whispering that
she was always there, waiting for me to walk from the old house to
the life that finally called her down. It is nonsense to say this, to say
she was here before she was here, the nonsense of language itself, how
bp nichol taught that to speak to phrases was to speak to saints. We
mourned him not for his work; we mourned the passing of the kind of
man he was. My daughter prays in the darkness, and the gibberish of
the martyrs pours from her unschooled lips. *Lul,* she says, *lul lul:
someone will come.* And it is me.

Let us romanticize shit. Yesterday's dinner, diaper curled away from pelvis like the petals of a tiger lily, examined shit, yes, today everything is working thank you. Speaking from the gut, we are successful parents; let us say the new diaper is a fresh page. It will hold the question posed by a magnificent poem, say the whole half-truth of literature itself — surely the analogy is at hand, though it comes far removed from the body worshipped by the brooding bachelors of Academy and Romance. But consider how a good firm shit is a sign this past resembled the past before it, the future will be good, the gods smiled and we loved well when we sent the invitation of a fertile egg. So far our daughter has nothing to regret which is why we mourn every stage that brings her closer to us; at the same time we mark up one more without trauma (so we say), her inimitable smell seizing consciousness through the nose and writing in big letters on the brain, you must change your kid.

Time to divine, this angry day,
exceptional sorrow at the airport:

my angels are in the air —
go my chick, my darling, my little one

already in this book, your birth,
empty mouth, first word,

This morning you said:
Dju djya dijy oobah pakh owp wooah

which Spell Checks out to:
D'au deja die obey a path own woe oath

Take it from there.

The manoeuvre makes asking
what you meant impossible.

Which becomes the essence of praise in certain circles.

Sophisticates in this business
disdain emotion, yet content allows the poem
to end.

In science fiction (Imaginative Fiction, sorry) emotion
defeats the robots when they take it internally
which logic tells them they must.

In the perfect language poem the act of reading alone
is the experience that makes the line work. Something like

The first word in this sentence is also the.

Some days I want to be made of metal,
like the plane that swallowed you and took off —

shiny metal without this lump in my gullet,
Window seat, over the wing.

I read aloud *Baby Dumbo was born in the Spring and his mother was proud, but oh, what big ears he had!* And Emma throws up her arms, saluting the magnificent ears of Dumbo, ears that make him a clown in the circus, which he hates, ears that get him back (somehow) to his elephant self via the mimicking of birds. There's a lot in there about talent and the freak, and I'm concerned, like all parents become concerned on contact with *what am I saying?* Would Dumbo be any *less* an elephant if he *couldn't* fly? Lennon sang *They didn't want me so they made me a star*, but Dumbo's mother *does* want him though she is taken from the narrative after the third page. (In the movie she fights the designs of men, is labelled mad and chained; Lennon's mother was killed by an off-duty cop driving drunk, and both mothers become songs that haunt the evenings of their sons.) But this is how his story always starts when the hero is a man, a man begins alone....Emma throws up her arms at the sight of him, decoding his picture the way D=U=M=B=O is decoded, this Disno-glyph, lost child, Emma's hands saying what her mouth cannot, already lifting him from the page, *Dumbo! So big! I know you!*

Alal dura tduh
el dorado
duck pond
city of the gift
of words —
5000 tongues
and she is chosen
by Canadian.
We hear
what we can make,
and for her, now
tduh is the sound
I make when *I* say
duck
when I say *that's right,*
duck,
the treasures of talk
are refined from non-talk.
Right before our eyes
in the alchemy of the mouth
we are led
to gold.

So much I've filled my father and my mother up with words
they have become descriptions of themselves.

I promise this page this book will end when Emma remembers
and remembering, gives names.

Silently today she stacks three hollow blocks of Duplo one by one
on the foundation of a longer block before her.

Silently, as in, *an achievement of the body*, her self as yet
unspoken, undoubled by her tongue's utterance of *I* —

sign of that which thinks, unperceived perceiver, precursor
of pure reason and its result: master, slave, self, syllable by syllable

built by language in the hollows of her mouth, current theory says,
so language can be used.

Into her silent body I've read the *I* I've already made of myself.
If she can *mean nothing* (if that is an ideal), it is not to me.

Right now, a silent baby places her toys in order while her father
watches outside her field of vision, and writes, now,

years away from the moment she can read this page and tell me
if I kept my word.

The puck is dropped. Naming begins: *this is a puck. Puh* she replies, *puh* she whispers. There are only so many apologies, so many startings over.

This is one, a baby at thirteen months saying *puh,* holding the flat hard face to her face, her breath sketching itself in the winter air against the new moon in her mittened hand.

After confession and prayer, the slate is wiped clean for the truly repentant, this is how I understand it, how it is mocked by the lie and faith reasoned in a circle.

The puck participates in both the sphere and the cube. I slide it down the grey sheet of ice like a curler with first rock. On this ice I can teach something new about force and motion.

Puh, she says and points. *Let's go get it* I say. *Let's go!* Every year the ice, new like the fresh page, conception, birth, a life converted mid-sentence; we say *has seen the light*

If the earth were just that bit further from the sun (say the planet was a human head, I mean the length a hair grows overnight) it would be winter everywhere, and Christ in buried Jerusalem would have said

this is the water upon which I build my church.

byobja durdur bagoo myemma
yesterday she taught me,

me making each sound
as I've written it here,

her saying it again back
to me. That's patience,

my daddy lips clumsy around
the delicacies of her catlike larynx,

tiny tongue; the poetry is
what her words say about language.

byobja durdur bagoo myemma
It was only last week

her jaw popped open, slapped shut
on single syllables, and

bha was *banana, Big Bird,*
bottle, bye-bye.

I said *bha* is the word for *banana,* or
bha is the first word in *banana.*

But *bha*
for *banana*

was not identical with *bha* for *Big Bird;*
under *b* in my alphabet

she built a pillar where
consonance and rhyme became one.

Today she says *eye kree*,
meaning *ice cream*
and gets a bowl full.

The rewarded exchange of
special sound for specific object,

and she starts the sentence
we have both been working for

behind the massy sound
where she begins.

It will be the sentence
that pushes me from a book

where I start a poem with
byobja durdur bagoo myemma

and take into myself the power
of nonsense spoken aloud.

But she is learning names and their use
and the first of these teaches

that everyone at once
lives in the crease

between "I" and "remember."

Her word for what she is now
is *bibi* —

call her language that, *bibi*,
as yet unrestrained by the words

of her parents but reaching for them
as if they never led her false.

Byobja durdur bagoo myemma. Eye kree.
is what it says:
Dada learning bibi.

April arrives, and the word
cusp determines this writing
the way the string of a genetic code
plays the cells: *cusp* — itself and another
at the same time, signs of the zodiac
sharing their feet on the calendar,
seasons not fixed, snow on the green
new grass; *the continuum is the single
greatest problem for Western thought,*
the problem obdurate and loved. Emma
picks up *Good Night Moon* and says to no one *Moon,*
the way she points to every crescent on the weather channel,
moon, moon, her body arcing from the sofa,
finger pointing so she too becomes the curl of
a planet that's caught the light:
it is April. The second syllable arrives. Clearly as her tongue
and jaw allow "pasta" whispers out *pah-pah.*
In sign she can decide between *"more please"*
and *"I'm finished,"*
and in the dark of the early morning room she strings
the baubles of sound together, and perhaps
it is the voices of Pinkybear, Tiny, Eeyore and Dolly
who live with her in the crib each night;
perhaps there is already a theatre and she
is on the lip of the stage.

where she
Emma
Hemma
answers the question
where's Emma?
by pointing in the mirror.
Who's that?
Hemmma
who's learning the alphabet
and recognizes the signs
auwa
deirja
dee —
who's that again?
Hemma
And where is Emma?
She points in the mirror,
but says nothing when
I point to her and ask
who's this?
herself unsigned
by herself —
that moment before it's lost
of Eve in Paradise
and Narcissus headlong for
transformation gazing
at the not-themselves
with more name
than the viewer.
I can ask,
where's an A?
and she peels

the little *A* sticker off the page,
places it on her overalls.
What's this letter?
Hh-aey-yee she says
breaking what masquerades
in the adult system
as a single phoneme:
continuing this way,
she is covered with letters,
I, R, G, D, B
and looking for more
by name; who's this?
Emma
Hemma
HimmHer
what she doesn't yet know
mirrored to her,
her Emmage
shimmering in the glass,
alphabet ready to receive.

What she said when she pointed to the birthmark on Lisa's face
was *moon*. 478 days old and the fields of her language overlap
below the eye, above the corner of her mother's mouth. The child sees
that the line begins in the arm. From our faces she knows eye, teeth,
nose; from books she knows moon, sheep, lion, and then this which no
one taught, though it is no less miraculous than looking at a yellow
disc on a blue page and saying *moon*, than pointing to a gibbous glow
and saying *moon*. And yet the tiny dark moon pulls the tide of the eye
towards itself again as Lisa speaks of this single syllable at the tip of
her baby's finger.
Everyone I tell this story to as the story of Emma's First Poem
agrees though still I doubt the claim to first, my baby authoring all
this time without intent, guiding the reader the way she takes my
hand when we walk. From the birth to the syllable to the line, she
is talking about us, and every day we are more like parents, inside
the words.

before she could walk
She sang before she could speak
She made a poem before she could utter a sentence

First word she says when
I walk into her room the morning of
May 1st is *mmeee*; she points to
the middle of her chest, uses *me*
correctly now as if overnight
the problem of this word
every speaker uses for itself
but isn't what you call them
she solved in her sleep
the way they say a writer
or a mathematician
goes to bed with a puzzle
and wakes up with an equation
or a song; *me* I've been saying,
pointing to me,
me, she's been saying,
pointing to me,
no, I've been saying,
Emma, I am me, then I take her hand gently
turn its language towards her,
because what I am about to say
is the only way I know to speak the truth
and contradicts itself completely:
you are me:
without the body outside the words
language collapses.

This morning she grasps it
in the sunrise, *me*
as her compass, its north
its own centre, its south
everyone else, grasps it and steers
out into the world farther
than she's gone to date: *good morning*
(and a little good-bye) I say
and she, showing off this new thing,
an invention that feels like discovery
between the tip of her finger
and the surface of her pyjama top, she smiles
up and says *me* again and again: *yes*
I say, I agree
confirming with the very words until
yesterday a correction:
that's you.

When she gestures *give me that* with her extended arm
pointing first to *that*, as she usually does to indicate
the object, and then continues the motion to point herself out
for the first time in sequence, she leaps millions of years
ahead of her tongue, and her tongue is poised to follow her arm
the way the reader follows the line on a conventional page,
ignoring the fragmentary nature of its evidence. Eons will vanish
in a word. For now the sentence begins
where the arm bends inwards, and *that* and *me,* once two
things whole and complete in themselves become vocabulary
in the muscular articulation of desire. The body entered the world
when two daughter cells did not break apart
but remained connected, behaved as one: this
is the foundation of metaphor. It arrives
on my doorstep that all knowledge is knowledge of the body,
that this isn't true, that in a poem nothing has to be. Everything
she's done to date has operated without reference,
but the sentence of the self is printed where
the tip of her finger meets the cloth above her breastbone.

Words evolve as species do. *Kwi-kwi* she said, and *kwi-kwi* became my
beacon. *Kwi-kwi* — she pointed to the crackers on the table the day
my father came to visit, *kwi-kwi* then *qua qua*, then *cwakoo* over the
7 days father and daughter and son dwelt together. In my house, I saw
my father with my baby, loving the baby to the limit of his powers.
Still he never left behind the violences of his poverty in Northern
England before the war, or the jungle battles he fought for the dying
Empire that took him at his word. I saw them in the small ferocities of
his gestures, the jabbing hand he used to make his point. He loved
language, but words alone were never enough. The baby learned to do
her first somersault that week, tucked in her chin, rested her palms on
the carpet and pushed. And she was proud and the parents were
proud and happy and *qua qua* became *cwakoo* in her mouth though
kwi-kwi had done just fine, the somersaulting baby saying *cwakoo* for
cracker the way some say the egg of a small and agile reptile hatched
the first awkward, eager bird and changed the world — not the way a
line is drawn across a beach or through a classic novel, but leapingly
— and I have put away that deafening hand I feared as a child though
I put aside also receiving the kind of love I feel for him the Bible
accurately predicts.

wyo, she says, pointing again to the wire that hangs from the wall once linked an intercom between this child's room and the bedroom of her parents. *Yes, it's a wire* I say, pointing as well where the ear of the machine used to listen in the night, and she turns the sound over and over — *wyo wyo wyo wayo whyo whyuh* — mouthing its texture, its own demands to shape her lips and tongue. These are the narrowing days: she specifies, discards, retains, practices, she pans for words among sound: *whyo* she offers the way she reaches towards my mouth with a bite of whatever I have given her to eat and we partake together what it is to provide. Before dinner yesterday she rolled to the edge of the couch, struck her head on the corner of a laundry basket, and we asked ourselves, over and over, how *could* we let that happen, but it ended with her in our arms the way we have come to count on comforting her when the fact of comfort is a wonder at all. Hours later, my father-in-law enters the room of events he did not see. She says *Pah-pah*, her name only for him. She points first to the couch, then to the basket (which we have moved) then in her eye the story.

I have built my life around the sentence, and this book follows.

The sentence makes possible the struggle for power.

From the Latin *sentire*, to think: "A sentence, therefore I am."

The atom of prose has split my house.

I have assumed her sentence will be a *no* to my own, and I want her to understand the power of her *no*, her refusal of food, of a kiss.

But I have not predicted the end of these pages on *Read book.*

If the world began with a word, it escapes its own sentence by birth.

Speak your life, beloved,

unpunctuated writing has no end

Acknowledgements

Gladly I owe a great debt to the people who supported me during the writing of this book, support expressed in editorial suggestions, encouragement, and when it was needed, their financial help. To Lisa Rouleau, Allan Markin, Jackie Flanagan, and the Markin-Flanagan Committee, my colleagues in the English Department at the University of Calgary, Isabel Henniger, Janis Svilpis, Gloria Toole, John Koch, the editorial collective of *filling station* magazine, Wendy Phillips, Nicole Markotić, Peter Oliva, Robert Hilles, Nadine McInnis, and my parents, Ralph and Doreen Harrison, my deepest thanks.

Biographical Notes

Richard Harrison's previous books are *Fathers Never Leave You, Recovering the Naked Man,* and *Hero of the Play.* During the writing of *Big Breath of a Wish,* he was the Canadian Writer-in-Residence at the University of Calgary under the Markin-Flanagan Distinguished Writers Program. He now teaches English and Creative Writing at Mount Royal College in Calgary where he lives with his wife Lisa Rouleau and their four-year-old daughter, Emma.

Emma Reine Harrison Rouleau was born on December 10, 1994 in Toronto. The poems in this book begin before her birth and follow her own invention/discovery/refinement of language until the age of two. Her insistence on creating speech out of every human sound she could make tested and expanded her father's ideas about words and their poetry. These days she's collaborating with her parents in making up stories, and she continues to argue about their endings.

Notes

John Lennon is quoted in "B'da" from "God," and in "Dumbo" from "I Found Out." Both songs from *John Lennon/Plastic Ono Band*.

The sketch referred to in "Derridad" is the centrepiece of Derrida's essay "R (into the bargain)" from *The Truth in Painting*, Geoff Bennington & Ian McLeod (trans). U of Chicago Press: Chicago. 1987.

I owe the epigraph to "V is for Block" to Mary di Michele, who extended her closed hand over the table in our creative writing class. She said, "John Cage says, 'Sound is the soul of objects released.'" Then she rapped the table.

The lines by Stan Lee & John Buscema in "Heroic Proportion" are from *How to Draw Comics the Marvel Way*. Simon & Schuster: New York. 1978.

The unattributed italicized lines in "Tomato, or So the Way of the World" are quoted from "Torso of an Archaic Apollo" by Rainer Maria Rilke with a slight variation on the translation by C. F. MacIntyre (*Rilke: Selected Poems*, U of California Press, 1962).

Ward Maxwell is quoted in "*Bulonga bloo*, or Basic Need," from his folio of poems, "No, I don't think it had a title," Peterborough, 1983.

The fourth line in "The D'Au" is a variation on Betsy Struthers' beautiful opening line of "L'Envoi, 1919" from *Censored Letters*. Mosaic Press: Oakville. 1984.

What Ross Leckie said to me years ago about "the continuum" is quoted in "Between Intention & Expression." I can hear him like it was yesterday.